MW00917562

MEDITERRANEAN
MEAL PREP
COOKBOOK

Delicious, Quick and Easy Recipes to Prep,
Grab and Go for Busy People

Jennifer Tate

TABLE OF CONTENTS

INTRODUCTION

Bringing together authentic recipes from Mediterranean countries, you will find all it takes to re-create some of the best Mediterranean meals in this cookbook.

Fresh, healthy, and easy to make...these are the best words to describe recipes within this Mediterranean cookbook.

You can choose from Mediterranean-style delicious meat recipes, bread and refreshing salads, seafood, and poultry.

We know, and this is precisely why we've prepared this **excellent book of Mediterranean Meal Prep recipes to save your time and money.**

The Mediterranean meals are refreshing and contain vitamins, minerals, and healthy fats. Besides being enjoyable, Mediterranean meals are also very healthy for you. Not only will you be able to enjoy quality food, but you will also improve your health. Obesity, diabetes, and heart disease are modern health issues practically unknown in the Mediterranean countries. The key in their diet is that they consume fresh and healthy ingredients, combined with a Mediterranean way of life – enjoying a lot of sun, their famous siesta, and a glass of red wine with the family and good friends.

Basic guidelines of the Mediterranean diet are:

- **Eat fish and seafood**
- **Include fresh herbs and spices**
- **Eat vegetables and fruits, both raw and cooked**
- **Focus on whole grains**
- **Use olive oil as the primary cooking oil**

This Mediterranean cookbook will take you on a culinary journey through Mediterranean countries while sharing tested recipes for healthy Mediterranean eating.

We suggest that you cook in bulk. Preparing meals for a week ahead is much easier than it sounds! With our recipes and recommendations and just a couple hours of cooking, you can provide a healthy and tasty diet! Moreover, it's not a secret that meals, nuts, grains, vegetables, seeds, and even meat are often cheaper to buy in bulk, and this is precisely what you can do with Mediterranean Meal Prep.

This book of recipes is your key to the world of faster, cheaper, and healthier cooking that will please your body and give you some spare time and money. Enjoy our well-tried dishes, and don't hesitate to come up with your own ideas. Bon Appetito!

MEDITERRANEAN DIET

THE MAGIC OF THE MEDITERRANEAN DIET

The Mediterranean diet, also called the Crete diet, is a nutritional concept. It is, therefore, a balanced mixed diet based on whole food consumption. The "Mediterranean diet" is a food selection and preparation just as it was in the Mediterranean in the 1950s and 1960s, especially among the rural population in olive cultivation areas, e.g., in Crete.

- *The main foods are fish, fresh fruit and vegetables, unsaturated fatty acids from olive oil, small quantities of meat, dairy products of sheep's milk or goat's milk, and moderate red wine consumption.*

Foods do not contain additives because the products are purchased fresh and are predominantly unprocessed. This diet is healthy and especially good for the heart and cardiovascular system.

Since the traditional "Mediterranean diet" is not just a diet but a way of life, there is no solid diet plan. You do not need to go hungry on this diet; you never will.

- *However, attention should be paid to daily calorie intake because only by reducing the calories (negative energy balance) can you reduce body weight in the long term.*

The term "Mediterranean" does not only reflect a dietary habit, but it means a way of life with particular importance on physical activity, periods of siesta, family and social contacts, and a stress-free lifestyle in harmony with nature.

How to prepare the daily menu is left to everyone. There is a variety of choices of possible dishes. Choosing between hot and cold, richer and less calorie-rich meals is possible. **The characteristic of this food is the high proportion of fruit, (wild) vegetables, bread, cereal products, potatoes, legumes, nuts, and seeds. The main fat supplier is olive oil.**

If you want to lose weight with this nutrition change, you should avoid the consumption of oil and fat as much as possible, as well as avoid fat sausage, fat cheese, and sweets.

- *The daily menu includes dairy products, mainly yogurt and cheese made from sheep or goat's milk.*

The consumption of dairy products is small compared to that in Central Europe.

- *On the menu is also plenty of fish. Meat from poultry is more frequently consumed than so-called "red" meat, but still in moderation. A moderate red wine variety is also allowed. When red wine is drunk, it is always consumed with lunch or dinner, but only one glass, no more.*

Most of the food comes from the region. Seasonal, fresh, mostly unprocessed foods are preferred because fewer additives are absorbed with this diet. **It is a carbohydrate-enhanced diet, with which the daily-recommended dietary fiber content**, according to the DGE, can be easily reached by 30 grams. The average total feed rate is 35%, but predominantly monounsaturated fatty acids and low-saturated fatty acids are absorbed. This nutritional formula contains a high proportion of vitamins, minerals, and secondary metabolites, all of which play an increasingly important role in today's diet.

The nutritional concept of the so-called "Mediterranean diet" is popular among nutritionists as one of the healthiest diets ever. It is suitable as a mixed food for a long-term diet. It is very balanced due to its high vitamin and mineral content.

- *It is suitable for a slow and healthy weight loss if the daily calorie quantity (negative energy balance) is lowered. The Mediterranean diet may also positively affect Diabetes Type 2 and cardiovascular disease.*

Numerous studies show that Mediterranean people are less affected by prevailing civilization diseases such as cardiovascular disease, hypertension, and obesity. Their secret is largely due to a balanced and healthy diet, including lots of vegetables, olive oil, and fresh fish. We have summarized for you the five essential elements of healthy cuisine around the Mediterranean diet.

- **Fruits and vegetables for every occasion**

Salad as an appetizer, vegetables as a side dish, and fruit for dessert... In the Mediterranean countries, there is no meal without fresh fruit and vegetables. Whether vitamin C, B or A, magnesium or zinc, fruits and vegetables provide micronutrients that play an essential role in all areas of our health. So do not hesitate to consume apple to zucchini because *the more colorful the selection, the greater the variety of vitamins, minerals, and phytochemicals!*

- **Plenty of legumes**

Legumes – such as beans, lentils, chickpeas, etc. – are an integral part of the Mediterranean diet and can be used in various combinations, herbs, and spices. In salads, soups, and stews, as a main dish, garnish, dip, or sauce, *legumes are a good source of high-quality vegetable protein and complex carbohydrates,* which in the form of softening fibers stimulate the digestion, prevent obesity, and reduce the risk of illness.

- **Vegetable oils**

Olive oil is found in every Mediterranean household and is used for almost all dishes and preparations. *The values in the olive oil are its mono- and poly-unsaturated fatty acids.* Omega-3 fatty acids, in particular, have a positive effect on the cardiovascular system since they improve the flow properties of the blood, reduce blood pressure, and have an anti-inflammatory effect. But also, linseed oil, rapeseed oil, and hemp oil are among the top candidates for healthcare products.

- **Lots of herbs**

Rosemary, basil, coriander... Herbs are omnipresent in Mediterranean cuisine and lend many dishes to their particular flavor. *Their healthy compounds and essential oils stimulate metabolism, promote digestion, and relieve inflammation.* In combination with garlic, these popular herbs are particularly beneficial because they act as an antibacterial, keep the vessel walls elastic, and prevent cholesterol deposits in the arteries. Generously seasoned dishes are not only delicious but also require less sea salt.

- **More fish than red meat**

Fresh fish is one of the treasures of the Mediterranean. Fish and seafood provide high-quality protein that is easily digestible and does not pollute the body. Valuable omega-3 fatty acids and minerals such as iodine and zinc protect against inflammation, strengthen the immune system, and promote brain function.

And finally...

Enjoy your daily meals with a genuine Mediterranean mentality - relaxed and to the fullest. It means you must take time, eat slowly, enjoy your food, and feel its energy. Also, several small portions, often in the warm Mediterranean regions, relieve the body. *This makes you feel lighter and more comfortable.*

MEDITERRANEAN SPICES AND HERBS

Mediterranean dishes are distinctive and flavorful, thanks to the use of quality and rich spices and herbs.

What would Mediterranean cuisine be without rosemary, thyme, basil, and other aromatic herbs? Herbs provide excellent taste, are also very healthy, and can easily be used as an alternative to sea salt.

Garlic:

- Taste: sharp and very powerful, intense
- Fits well with: soups, sauces, steaks, and stews

Basil:

- Flavor: spicy, peppery-spicy, slightly sweetish note
- Fits well with: tomatoes, aubergines, peppers, and the resulting dishes such as tomato soup; also salads, stews, mussels, and egg dishes

Rosemary:

- Flavor: herb-spicy, slightly bitter
- Fits well with: poultry, strong meat, and lamb dishes

Sage:

- Taste: spicy-bitter, balsamic odor
- Fits well with: salads, poultry, tomatoes, minestrone, and mince

Thyme:

- Taste: spicy tart flavor
- Fits well with: vegetable soup, spaghetti sauces, tomato salad, mushroom dishes, omelets, and potatoes

Oregano:

- Taste: spicy, tart, and slightly bitter
- Fits well with: fish, sheep's cheese, tomato soup, carrots, vegetables, and pizza

Mint:

- Taste: uniquely fresh, menthol-containing
- Fits well with: sauces, pea soup, potatoes, and especially desserts

Tarragon:

- Taste: piquant-tart and slightly peppery taste
- Fits: soups, fish, salads, and sauces

Coriander:

- Taste: very peculiar, mildly peppery, slightly sweet, either one likes it, or one does not - who does not like it describes the taste as unpleasantly soapy

- Fits well with: poultry, salads, pies, cakes, carrots, and pickled fruits

Spices and herbs are of great importance in Mediterranean cuisine because the composition of spices makes the dishes of the Mediterranean kitchen create exceptional taste experiences!

Mediterranean cuisine cannot be imagined without certain spices and herbs! Basil is one of the most essential Mediterranean spices. The noble and slightly peppery flavor of the basil makes it an absolute must in Mediterranean cuisine. The best-known use for basil is Pesto a la Genovese, which is made up of basil of pine nuts, garlic, parmesan, and plenty of olive oil. For a long time, basil was known as a pizza herb, but soon oregano replaced it.

Oregano, like basil, is one of the most famous spices for Mediterranean cuisine, and both are used in combination with seasoning. As a single spice, oregano is famous in Italy for its use on hot, beloved pizza. In Greece, on the other hand, it is often seasoned with dried oregano, such as, for example, sheep's cheese or olives. Also, the spicy Greek peasant salad and hearty meat dishes, such as gyros or souvlaki, give the oregano its unique taste! We also offer mixed spice mixes such as our pizza, sheep cheese, and gyro spices.

- *The combination of fresh ingredients, dried spices, and herbs makes Mediterranean cuisine incomparable!*

Many believe that fresh spices have a more intense flavor than dried spices. The Mediterranean cuisine is proof that dried spices can taste just as aromatic and intense, if not even more intensively, than fresh spices. These Mediterranean spices include oregano, thyme, and bay leaves. Surely, you know the incredible aromatic flavor of rosemary. **The dry seasoning has a much more intense and aromatic taste than the fresh spice.** Rosemary should, therefore, be eaten sparingly when cooking since otherwise, the flavor can quickly turn into bitterness. Rosemary is very popular in Mediterranean cuisine, especially Italian cuisine, and is part of different Mediterranean spice mixes, such as Italian Blend.

WHY MEDITERRANEAN MEAL PREP?

Mediterranean Meal Prep is a new cooking trend that has every reason for the enormous global popularity recently gained. The basic idea is that you **cook your meals a week ahead**.

Why is that so cool? - In brief, **Mediterranean Meal Prep saves your health, money, time, and nerves.**

The first is rather obvious: premade Mediterranean meals are just as good for your health and fitness as any other Mediterranean meal. Let's take a closer look at the other three.

WHY IS MEAL PREP CHEAPER THAN USUAL COOKING?

In fact, there are several reasons, and there is hardly anyone in the world who won't find at least one that is relevant to them:

It is always cheaper to buy in bulk. On the other hand, many healthy ingredients can be repurposed for several meals, so you don't have to worry that leftovers will get lost and rotten in the fridge. This way, with a well-planned week-long menu, you can feel free to go for bigger pack deals and daily promotions and buy more and cheaper ingredients that you know you will use.

Moreover (and probably none of you will challenge that), when there are **some delicious and no-time-to-cook meals waiting for you** in your fridge, the temptation to run by a fast-food restaurant, order a pizza or get a takeaway is much smaller than when you still have to go and grab some products in a shop and then spend another half an hour in the kitchen.

Altogether, this makes the cost per meal with Mediterranean Meal Prep really much cheaper than without it.

HOW DOES MEDITERRANEAN MEAL PREP SAVE YOUR TIME?

This is not so obvious, especially at the very beginning. It's particularly hard to believe when you are planning the first week's menu and start cooking all of it for the first time. Frankly speaking, it's quite a lump of time, and you may easily get disheartened even before you have finished cooking for the first week (especially before you have finished cooking for the first week). However, with this wonderful recipe book, the issue of planning has been solved for you. As for the time cooking, the experience of those who have already discovered the magic ease of Mediterranean Meal Preps shows that once it's settled into a groove, cooking meals for a week will take no more than an hour or two. "Two hours!" you might think skeptically, but two hours per seven days a week is just 17 minutes for each day - we bet you are now spending more time on your cooking!

HOW DOES MEAL PREP SAVE YOUR NERVES?

And last but not least is saving your nerves. First, **you don't have to worry about cooking breakfast in the morning**. You can spend more time sweetly dreaming or having a pleasant lie-in instead of rushing to the cooker.

Moreover, the fewer things you worry about during the day, the better and more confident you feel. So, remove all those thoughts about where to buy food and how to find time and energy for cooking after work. Knowing that there is something tasty and (what's even more important) ready for your meal definitely makes it one less problem to bother about.

HOW TO STICK TO MEDITERRANEAN MEAL PREP?

You've already tried a couple of modern food trends. Bright-eyed and bushy-tailed at the beginning, somewhat tired and bored in the middle, and finally distressed and disappointed with the trend that hasn't managed to become a life-changer and yourself, who has given up a supposedly useful habit... again. First, let us tell you one thing - you are not the only one like that. To be honest with you, we've all been through that. And this is precisely why we have prepared some tips on how not to get tired of Mediterranean Meal Prep and stick to it.

- Add some scheduling at the start

Initially, it's essential to embed bulk cooking into your daily routines. **Schedule a couple of hours at the weekend** and set a reminder in your calendar to ensure that you don't end up remembering your plan to start meal prep on a busy Monday morning. It's not that easy at the start, but as you get further and see all the advantages of pre-made meals, this will feel like a delighting possibility rather than a boring chore.

Don't do it all at once.

Sometimes too much eagerness at the beginning is not exactly for good. It might be worse to introduce Mediterranean Meal Prep into your life step by step. Why don't you start with breakfast? Most of us already have a habit of eating more or less overlapping meals in the mornings. **Prepare your first meals of the day and enjoy some extra time in bed**. Then you can replace your what-should-I-eat lunches with preplanned and pre-cooked dishes, and then when you are already familiar with buying and cooking in bulk, it can be high time to switch to premade dinners.

- ### Don't make everything from scratch.

Mediterranean Meal Prep is about healthy eating, but that doesn't mean you have to start your own kitchen garden and raise chicken in the backyard. Of course, you can if you want to, but pre-peeled vegetables and cut meat are still there for you. **Don't be afraid to ease your prep!**

- ### Don't get yourself bored.

Look through the recipes in our book before planning your menu and realize that you don't have to eat the same stuff every day. In fact, moving to Mediterranean Meal Prep is **a great chance to vary your diet**. You might not have imagined how many different and delicious meals can be cooked from more or less the same set of overlapping ingredients.

- ### Get a company

Getting good company is a great way not to give up and make Mediterranean Meal Preps cooking more fun. Don't you have a friend or two who also would like to make their life more comfortable and healthier? Get them in! Plan, buy and cook the Preps together to enjoy both opportunities of cheaper no-stress meals and time with your friends.

Having passed all the way from Mediterranean Meal Prep newbies not knowing where to start to experienced premade food chefs looking forward to cooking some delicious meals for the week to come, we have collected some more great tips for you to make your way even smoother and happier.

- Renew your container park

Storing pre-made meals can become a pain in the neck if you don't have enough convenient containers. Just imagine sticking foods in pans on plates and then trying to get them all in the fridge - isn't that a disaster. Don't make it hard on yourself; invest in several microwave and dishwasher compatible container sets. This one-time investment will return to you with lots of saved time and space.

- Get your multicooker out

Multicooker can really be of huge help when it comes to Mediterranean Meal Prep. Soups, sauces, casseroles, and other slow-cooked meals can make a big part of your prep diet. Just toss all the ingredients in the cooker and feel free to do some other thing, watch a film or lie on a sofa enjoying weekend laziness while your food is getting ready. Cool it down and store it in the fridge.

- Shape your basic menu

As you make and try different meals, pay attention to how you feel about them. Have you really liked it? Have you got tired of some ingredients by the end of the week? What has been the best meal of the week? Which dish has been a failure? Repeat the best pieces in other week's menus and diversify them, adding some new meals. This way, you will not only be sure to find something you will definitely like but eventually get some core recipes that you can always rely on. Finally, you will probably even memorize those and will be able to buy the necessary ingredients and cook them without any aid.

- Arrange theme days

For some of us, making a menu may be more difficult than cooking food. If this is the case, theme days may become an excellent solution for you! For example, make Monday a seafood day, Tuesday a poultry day, Wednesday a veggie day, etc. This is not necessary, but it can make planning your menu easier.

- Look at your weekly planner before you plan the menu

Not every week is the same. Take a second and run through your diary to ensure that you will not cook too much or too little for the following week. Are you going out with friends on Tuesday? Are you invited to a birthday party? Do you have an integration dinner at work on Friday? Don't let yourself be disappointed with leftover meals at the end of the week. No one wants to cook something that won't be eaten, which can dishearten you. On the other hand, check if someone is coming to your place. First of all, this is a great reason to try some of the more festive Mediterranean meals; on the other hand, you need to ensure that there will be enough for everyone.

- Use overlapping ingredients

Buying in bulk is always cheaper, so consider using the same ingredient for different meals: olives, carrots, onion, tomatoes... even meat can be bought once and used in many dishes. All you need to do is keep the list of ingredients from the previous day when planning the next one.

- Keep a stock of additives and seasonings

Coconut milk, hot chili sauce, mustard and vinegar, crushed tomatoes, olive oil, onions, garlic, fresh greens, and dried herbs - it's really cool to have something to give the final touch to your foods. A piece of soft cheese, some sour cream, fresh vegetable, or tomato sauce will also make your meal feel like a freshly cooked dish.

- Use an oven

Of course, it is faster to microwave the meal, but consider using an oven to heat the meals. In this case, you may collect the ingredients, slightly pre-cook them at the weekend, and then bake the meal in an oven to have a fast dinner.

- Don't be too strict with yourself

Life is life, and things happen. There is no way we can avoid it. Have you been unexpectedly invited on a date? A friend has come, and you've used the meals planned for tomorrow? There are promotions in a nearby steak restaurant, and you can't help ordering their juicy sirloin? - Don't worry. That's totally OK. Mediterranean Meal Preps are here to make your life easier and help you organize your meals most conveniently and healthily, but this doesn't mean that you must become a slave of your diet plan with no chance to step aside. It's not about blaming yourself, but rather about having a simple plan of getting back on trial the next day!

BREAKFAST

CYPRUS QUINOA BOWL

Servings: 6

Prep Time: 10 minutes

Cook Time: 20 minutes

INGREDIENTS:

½ tsp. of freshly ground pepper

1 tsp. of olive oil

5 oz. (140 g) of baby spinach

½ cup carrot, diced

½ cup (50 g) mushrooms, diced

1 cup (90 g) broccoli florets, boiled for 2 minutes

1 cup (118 g) of feta cheese

12 whole eggs

¼ cup (60 ml) of plain Greek yogurt

1 tsp. of onion powder

1 tsp. of garlic powder

½ tsp. of sea salt

2 cups (370 g) of cooked quinoa

STEPS:

1. Add your eggs, yogurt, onion powder, garlic powder, sea salt, and pepper to a large bowl. Whisk everything together.

2. Heat olive oil in a large skillet. Add your spinach and cook for 3–4 minutes, until the spinach is just wilted.

3. Add carrots, broccoli florets, and mushrooms. Cook for 5–10 minutes until they have softened.

4. Add your egg mixture. Cook for 7–9 minutes, constantly stirring, until the eggs have set and are scrambled.

5. Add your feta and quinoa. Cook for a few minutes to warm.

NUTRITIONAL INFORMATION (PER SERVING)

Calories: 357, Carbs: 20g, Protein: 23g, Fat: 20g, Fiber: 3g, Sugar: 4g

VEGETABLE QUICHE

Servings: 8

Prep Time: 15 minutes

Cook Time: 55 minutes

INGREDIENTS:

prepared pie crust	⅓ cup (40 g) crumbled feta cheese
1 cup (113 g) of shredded cheddar cheese	4 whole eggs
½ cup (60 g) of sun-dried tomatoes	1¼ cups (300 ml) of whole milk
1 diced onion (70 g)	1 tsp. of dried oregano
2 minced garlic cloves	1 tsp. of dried parsley
1 diced red bell pepper	2 tbsp. of butter
2 cups (60 g) of fresh spinach	sea salt, to taste
¼ cup (45 g) of sliced Kalamata olives	pepper, to taste

STEPS:

1. Boil a small pot of water.

2. Place your sun-dried tomatoes in a glass measuring cup. Pour your boiling water over them so that they are just covered. Let them sit for 5 minutes. Drain and chop.

3. Preheat your oven to 375°F (190°C). Place your pie crust on a pie plate. Flute the edges.

4. Melt butter in a skillet over medium-high heat. Add garlic and onion, and cook for 3 minutes, until the onions are tender. Add red pepper and cook for 3 more minutes, until the pepper is just tender.

5. Add spinach, olives, parsley, and oregano, and cook for 5 minutes until the spinach has wilted.

6. Remove from heat. Add in feta cheese and tomatoes. Mix everything well.

7. Spread your mixture into your pie crust.

8. Whisk eggs, milk, sea salt, pepper, and ½ cup of cheese in a bowl. Pour your mixture over the spinach mixture. Sprinkle it with the rest of the cheddar cheese.

9. Bake for 50–55 minutes. The crust should be golden brown, and the eggs should be set.

10. Remove your quiche from the oven, and let it cool for 10–15 minutes before serving.

NUTRITIONAL INFORMATION (PER SERVING)

Calories: 290, Carbs: 20g, Protein: 12g, Fat: 19g, Fiber: 3g, Sugar: 4g

FRENCH HASH

Servings: 4

Prep Time: 10 minutes

Cook Time: 24 minutes

INGREDIENTS:

2 diced sweet potatoes

1 chopped red onion

2 chopped garlic cloves

1 cup (134 g) of drained and rinsed canned green peas

1 lb. (450 g) of asparagus, chopped

4 whole eggs

1 tsp. of red wine vinegar

½ cup green onion, chopped

½ cup (60 g) of crumbled feta cheese

1½ tsp. of allspice

1 tsp. of dried oregano

1 tsp. of paprika

1 tsp. of coriander

olive oil

¼ tsp. of white sugar

sea salt, to taste

freshly ground pepper, to taste

STEPS:

1. Heat 1½ tablespoons of olive oil in a large skillet over medium-high heat. Add onions, garlic, and potatoes. Season with sea salt and pepper, and cook for 5–7 minutes, often stirring, until the potatoes are tender.

2. Add peas, asparagus, and another pinch or two of sea salt and pepper, along with the rest of your spices. Cook for 5–7 minutes. Reduce your heat to low, and stir regularly as you complete the following steps.

3. Bring a pot of water to a simmer and add 1 teaspoon vinegar. Break your eggs into a bowl. Stir the water, and gently transfer your eggs to the water. Cook for 3 minutes. Remove the eggs from the water and transfer them onto a kitchen towel. Season with sea salt and pepper.

4. Remove the potato hash from the heat and add red onions, feta, and parsley. Gently nestle your poached eggs in your hash.

NUTRITIONAL INFORMATION (PER SERVING)

Calories: 535, Carbs: 34.5g, Protein: 26.6g, Fat: 20.8g, Sugar: 6.9g

NUT GRANOLA WITH SEEDS

Servings: 6

Prep Time: 5 minutes

Cook Time: 5 minutes

INGREDIENTS:

½ cup (40 g) of oats

⅓ cup (30 g) of sliced almonds

2 tbsp. of sunflower seeds

1 tbsp. of flax seeds

2 tbsp. of shredded coconut

2 tbsp. of liquid honey

1 tsp. of cinnamon

1 tsp. of coconut oil

yogurt or milk, fruits (for serving)

STEPS:

1. Mix together all of your ingredients in a bowl.

2. Heat a nonstick pan over medium heat, and add your mixture. Cook for 3–5 minutes to toast, stirring frequently.

3. Remove from heat and let your granola cool. Serve with fruits and yogurt / milk.

NUTRITIONAL INFORMATION (PER SERVING)

Calories: 120, Carbs: 14g, Protein: 3g, Fat: 7g, Fiber: 2g, Sugar: 7g

BREAKFAST CASSEROLE

Servings: 8

Prep Time: 15 minutes

Cook Time: 1 hour

INGREDIENTS:

1 lb. (450 g) Italian turkey / chicken sausage, with casings removed

1 chopped onion (70 g)

5 oz. (140 g) of spinach

1 cup (240 ml) of milk

6 slices of whole-grain bread, cut into bite-sized pieces

1 cup (116 g) of sun-dried tomatoes

1 can (14 oz./400 g) of artichoke hearts, drained

½ cup (60 g) of crumbled feta cheese

8 whole eggs

½ tsp. of sea salt

2 tbsp. of olive oil

STEPS:

1. Heat 1 tablespoon of olive oil in a large skillet over medium-high heat. Add your sausage and cook for 8 minutes, breaking it up as you cook. Transfer the sausage to a paper towel.

2. Add another tablespoon of olive oil to your skillet. Add onion and sea salt. Cook for 5 minutes. Add spinach and cook for 1 minute.

3. Beat your eggs in a bowl and add milk. Add bread, sun-dried tomatoes, artichokes, feta, and sausage mixture.

4. Spray a baking dish with cooking spray.

5. Pour the mixture into a baking dish, cover, and refrigerate for at least 1 hour and up to overnight.

6. Preheat your oven to 350°F (176°C). Take out the casserole and let it sit for 30 minutes.

7. Bake for 45 minutes. Remove from the oven, and let it sit for 10 minutes before serving.

NUTRITIONAL INFORMATION (PER SERVING)

Calories: 366, Carbs: 23.9g, Protein: 28.2g, Fat: 14.5g, Fiber: 5.7g, Sugar: 6.7g

CREAMY VEGAN TOAST

Servings: 4

Prep Time: 10 minutes

Total Time: 10 minutes

INGREDIENTS:

4 slices of whole-grain bread

½ cup (125 g) of hummus

2 Tbsp. chickpeas

½ cup (50 g) mushrooms, cooked

6 slices of zucchini, grilled/baked

2 tbsp. of chopped olives

za'atar spice blend

a handful of basil

STEPS:

1. Toast your bread.

2. Spread 2 tablespoons of hummus on each slice of bread. Add a pinch or two of za'atar on top of each slice.

3. Load on the rest of your ingredients, and serve.

NUTRITIONAL INFORMATION (PER SERVING)

Calories: 166, Carbs: 29.4g, Protein: 6.1g, Fat: 4.2g, Sugar: 4.7g

NUTRITIOUS OVERNIGHT OATS

Servings: 1

Prep Time: 10 minutes

Total Time: 8 hours

INGREDIENTS:

½ cup (40 g) of old-fashioned rolled oats

½ cup (120 ml) of whole milk / water

2 tbsp. of chopped dates/bananas/berries

1 tbsp. of toasted pine nuts/almond flakes

1 tsp. of liquid honey

¼ tsp. of cinnamon

a pinch of sea salt

STEPS:

1. Mix oats, sea salt, and ½ cup of water/milk in a bowl. Cover and refrigerate overnight.
2. Heat the oats or serve cold. Top with the rest of your ingredients.

NUTRITIONAL INFORMATION (PER SERVING)

Calories: 282, Carbs: 48.2g, Protein: 6.7g, Fat: 8.9g, Fiber: 6.1g, Sugar: 18.7g

BREAKFAST SMOOTHIE BOWL

Servings: 1

Prep Time: 10 minutes

Total Time: 10 minutes

INGREDIENTS:

⅔ cup (100 g) of frozen raspberries

½ cup (75 g) of frozen sliced bananas

½ cup (120 ml) of unsweetened almond milk

5 tbsp. of sliced almonds

¼ tsp. of cinnamon

⅛ tsp. of cardamom

⅛ tsp. of vanilla extract

¼ cup of blueberries

1 tbsp. of unsweetened coconut flakes

STEPS:

1. Blend your raspberries, banana, milk, 3 tablespoons of almonds, cinnamon, vanilla, and cardamom until smooth.

2. Pour your smoothie into a bowl and sprinkle with coconut, the rest of your almonds, and blueberries.

NUTRITIONAL INFORMATION (PER SERVING)

Calories: 360, Carbs: 45.6g, Protein: 9.2g, Fat: 19g, Fiber: 14g, Sugar: 21.4g

TUSCAN CHICKEN SKILLET

Servings: 5

Prep Time: 10 minutes

Cook Time: 12 minutes

INGREDIENTS:

1 lb. (450 g) of chicken fillets, chopped

1 can (14 oz. / 400 g) of artichoke hearts, drained

½ cup (60 g) of sliced sun-dried tomatoes

1 can (15 oz. / 425 g) chickpeas, drained

½ cup of diced sweet potato

1 thinly sliced yellow onion (70 g)

2 minced garlic cloves

10 minced Kalamata olives

1 tbsp. of coriander

1 tbsp. of rosemary

1 tbsp. of oregano

1 tbsp. of paprika

STEPS:

1. Heat a cast-iron skillet over medium heat.

2. Add chicken fillets, and cook for 10 - 15 minutes until lightly browned.

3. Add chickpeas, sweet potato, garlic, onion, and sauté for 5 minutes, stirring often.

4. Add your coriander, artichoke hearts, and tomatoes, and cook for 5 minutes over medium-high heat.

5. Remove from heat, stir in your olives and herbs, and serve.

NUTRITIONAL INFORMATION (PER SERVING)

Calories: 360, Carbs: 28g, Protein: 22g, Fat: 18g, Sugar: 5g

EGG MUFFINS WITH SPINACH

Servings: 6

Prep Time: 20 minutes

Cook Time: 25 minutes

INGREDIENTS:

8 sheets of thawed phyllo (9x14 inches / 23x36 cm)

⅓ cup of diced red onion

6 whole eggs

10 oz. (280 g) of frozen chopped spinach, thawed and squeezed dry

½ cup (60 g) of crumbled feta cheese

½ cup (120 ml) of whole milk

¼ cup of chopped dill

½ tsp. of freshly ground pepper

¼ tsp. of sea salt

3 tbsp. of olive oil

STEPS:

1. Preheat your oven to 350°F (176°C). Spray a 12-cup muffin tin with cooking spray.

2. Heat 1 tablespoon of olive oil in a skillet over medium heat. Add onion and half of sea salt. Cook, often stirring, for 4 minutes. Remove from heat.

3. Whisk together eggs, spinach, milk, feta, pepper, dill, the rest of the sea salt, and cooked onions in a large bowl.

4. Lay out phyllo sheets, and cover them with a clean kitchen towel (to keep them from drying out).

5. Add 2 tablespoons of olive oil to a small bowl. Brush one sheet of phyllo with oil, and cut it into 6 pieces. Place one square in a muffin cup, and press it down gently. Place another square on top so that the edges overlap. Repeat for the rest of your phyllo.

6. Fill each cup with ¼ cup of your egg mixture.

7. Bake for 25–30 minutes.

NUTRITIONAL INFORMATION (PER SERVING)

Calories: 266, Carbs: 18.2g, Protein: 12.4g, Fat: 16.2g, Fiber: 2.1g, Sugar: 2.4g

ITALIAN FRITTATA

Servings: 8

Prep Time: 15 minutes | Cook Time: 30 minutes

INGREDIENTS:

1 chopped red bell pepper

1 small diced zucchini

2 chopped red onions (140 g)

4 oz. (113 g) of broccoli florets

7 whole eggs

¼ cup (60 ml) of whole milk

⅓ cup (40 g) of crumbled feta cheese, plus more for serving

⅓ cup of chopped parsley, plus more for serving

¼ tsp. of baking powder (optional)

sea salt

freshly ground pepper

4 tbsp. of olive oil

1 tsp. of fresh thyme

STEPS:

1. Preheat your oven to 450°F (232°C). Place a rimmed baking sheet in the oven and let it heat up a bit.

2. Mix bell peppers, zucchini, green onion, broccoli, 3 tablespoons of olive oil, and a pinch of sea salt and pepper in a bowl.

3. Remove the pan from the oven and arrange your veggie mixture on the pan. Place the pan back in the oven and cook for 15 minutes. Remove veggies from the oven.

4. Lower your heat to 400°F (205°C).

5. Whisk together eggs, baking powder (if using), milk, feta, parsley, thyme, and a pinch of sea salt and pepper.

6. Add veggies to your egg mixture, folding them in.

7. Add some oil to a cast-iron skillet and warm over medium-high heat. Pour your mixture into the skillet and cook for 2–3 minutes.

8. Transfer the pan to the oven and cook for 8–10 minutes. Remove from the oven.

9. Sprinkle with feta cheese and parsley.

NUTRITIONAL INFORMATION (PER SERVING)

Calories: 136, Carbs: 4.2g, Protein: 7.8g, Fat: 10.2g, Fiber: 1.1g

LUNCH & DINNER

BEEF AND RICE BOWLS

Servings: 4

Prep Time: 20 minutes

Cook Time: 15 minutes

INGREDIENTS:

1 lb. (450 g) of lean ground beef

5.3 oz. (150 g) of Greek yogurt

2 minced garlic cloves

1 tbsp. of olive oil

1½ tsp. of dried oregano

½ cucumber, chopped

½ cup (90 g) olives

2 cups (500 g) of cooked rice

1 tbsp. plus ¼ tsp. of dried dill

hummus, to taste

crumbled feta, to taste

pita wedges

sea salt, to taste

freshly ground pepper, to taste

Sriracha (optional)

STEPS:

1. Mix yogurt, chopped cucumber, olive oil, garlic, ¼ teaspoon dried dill, and a pinch or two of sea salt and pepper in a food processor. Pulse until everything is combined. Stick it in the fridge until you are ready to serve.

2. Add beef to a skillet and cook over medium-high heat, breaking it up as it cooks. Cook until the beef is done, with no remaining pink. Drain any excess fat.

3. Add remaining dried dill, a pinch of sea salt, oregano, olives, and a pinch of pepper.

4. Increase your heat to high and pour ⅔ cup water into the skillet. Bring to a boil, reduce heat to low, and let it simmer until the water has evaporated.

5. To serve, add ½ cup of rice to a bowl, spoon some beef on top, add some hummus and feta, and drizzle with your yogurt sauce and Sriracha (if using). Serve with pita wedges.

NUTRITIONAL INFORMATION (PER SERVING)

Calories: 472, Carbs: 35.7g, Protein: 34.4g, Fat: 20.3g, Fiber: 4.3g, Sugar: 3.9g

SALMON SALAD

Servings: 2

Prep Time: 15 minutes

Cook Time: 15 minutes

8 oz. (230 g) salmon fillets

1 tsp. of dried basil

½ tsp. of red pepper flakes

2 minced garlic cloves

1 cup (90 g) of broccoli florets

2 tbsp. of olive oil

2 cups (150 g) of chopped lettuce

a handful of fresh basil

1 tbsp. of lemon juice

10 pitted olives

2 tbsp. of hummus

sea salt, to taste

freshly ground pepper, to taste

STEPS:

1. Rub your salmon with dried basil, one minced garlic clove, and red pepper flakes.

2. Place lettuce in a bowl. Add basil, lemon juice, olive oil, and the rest of your minced garlic. Mix everything together and season with sea salt and pepper to taste. (For meal prepping the salad, you will want to mix the portion you are eating and keep the rest separated until you are ready to eat.)

3. Heat 1 tablespoon of olive oil in a nonstick pan. Add broccoli and cook for 2 minutes.

4. Transfer the broccoli to a plate and add salmon fillets to the pan, cooking over medium-high heat. Cover with a lid and cook for 6–7 minutes, flipping the salmon halfway through.

5. Arrange your salad. Place salad mixture in a bowl, add your olives, hummus, and broccoli, and top it off with salmon.

NUTRITIONAL INFORMATION (PER SERVING)

Calories: 580, Carbs: 20g, Protein: 38g, Fat: 40g, Fiber: 8g, Sugar: 4g

WARM LENTIL SALAD

Servings: 4

Prep Time: 10 minutes

Cook Time: 20 minutes

INGREDIENTS:

1⅓ cups (260 g) lentils, soaked

1 chopped tomato

3 sliced garlic cloves

2 minced garlic cloves

3 tbsp. of olive oil

½ tsp. of cumin

½ tsp. of coriander

½ tsp. of turmeric

1 tsp. of mint

1 tsp. of red pepper flakes

½ onion (35 g), chopped

a handful of spinach

sea salt, to taste

1 tbsp. of tahini

juice from 1 lime

1 diced cucumber

2 diced tomatoes

1 diced onion (70 g)

STEPS:

1. Add diced cucumber, tomatoes, onion, and 1 tablespoon of olive oil to a bowl, and mix well. Set aside.

2. Cook chopped onion, 1 tablespoon of olive oil, and 2 of your sliced garlic cloves in a pan over medium-high heat. Add spices and chopped tomato. Smash the tomato with a spatula after a few minutes of cooking.

3. Stir in your lentils. Season with sea salt and add about 1 cup of water to completely cover your lentil mixture. Cover with a lid and cook for 10–15 minutes.

4. Add spinach and cook for 5 more minutes. Add more water if needed.

5. Turn off the heat and add your remaining sliced garlic clove and another tablespoon of olive oil.

6. Mix tahini, lime juice, minced garlic, and a pinch of sea salt in a small bowl. Add 2–3 tablespoons of water until you reach your desired creaminess.

7. Arrange your bowl, and store the leftovers separately.

NUTRITIONAL INFORMATION (PER SERVING)

Calories: 208, Carbs: 19g, Protein: 7g, Fat: 13g, Fiber: 6g, Sugar: 4g

CAULIFLOWER RICE AND TURKEY

Servings: 2

Prep Time: 7 minutes

Cook Time: 13 minutes

INGREDIENTS:

6 oz. (170 g) ground turkey

3 cups (320 g) of cauliflower rice

1 chopped carrot

½ chopped red bell pepper

½ tsp turmeric

2 tsp paprika

1 tsp cumin

1 tbsp. of pickled jalapeños

½ tsp. of freshly ground pepper

1 tsp red pepper flakes

½ tsp coriander

2 tbsp. of olive oil

4 minced garlic cloves

sea salt, to taste

chopped herbs (optional for serving)

STEPS:

1. Cook your turkey in a pan with ¼ cup water over medium-high heat. Cover and cook for 4–5 minutes.

2. Add turmeric, pepper, red pepper flakes, cumin, coriander, 1 teaspoon of paprika, and 1 garlic clove. Stir for 2–3 minutes, or until all the water has evaporated.

3. Reduce heat to medium and stir in your cauliflower rice, carrot, bell pepper, 1 tablespoon of olive oil, the rest of your paprika, and a pinch of sea salt. Cook for 3–4 minutes.

4. Stir in the rest of the garlic, jalapeño, and 1 tablespoon of olive oil. Stir for 2 minutes, remove from heat, and serve with your fresh herbs.

NUTRITIONAL INFORMATION (PER SERVING)

Calories: 443, Carbs: 18g, Protein: 28g, Fat: 31g, Fiber: 7g, Sugar: 6g

CHICKEN SKILLET WITH VEGETABLES

Servings: 2

Prep Time: 8 minutes

Cook Time: 12 minutes

INGREDIENTS:

1½ cups chopped eggplant

8 oz. (230 g) boneless, skinless chicken thighs / chicken breast

2 chopped tomatoes

1 tsp. of tomato paste

1 chopped carrot

½ cup (50 g) of chopped broccoli florets

½ cup (90 g) of whole olives

2 garlic cloves

2 scallions

2 tbsp. of olive oil

½ cup (60 g) of crumbled feta cheese

1 tsp dried basil (or a handful of chopped fresh basil)

½ tsp coriander

½ tsp red pepper flakes (optional)

STEPS:

1. Cut your chicken into bite-sized pieces. Warm olive oil in a skillet over medium-high heat.

2. Add chicken and eggplant and cook for 4–5 minutes.

3. Add tomatoes, cover with a lid, and cook for 3 minutes.

4. Stir in tomato paste. Add 1–2 tablespoons of water, if needed.

5. Reduce heat to medium. Stir in broccoli, scallions, carrots, basil (if you are using dried basil), coriander, and red pepper flakes (if using). Add one more tablespoon of olive oil, and cook for 3–4 minutes.

6. Add feta cheese, olives, garlic, and basil (if you use fresh basil). Cook for 1 minute. Remove from heat.

7. Season with sea salt and pepper to taste, and serve.

NUTRITIONAL INFORMATION (PER SERVING)

Calories: 352, Carbs: 15g, Protein: 24g, Fat: 23g, Fiber: 5g, Sugar: 6g

CHICKPEA SKILLET

Servings: 2

Prep Time: 8 minutes

Cook Time: 7 minutes

INGREDIENTS:

1 can (15 oz. / 425 g) of chickpeas, rinsed and drained

4 chopped tomatoes

1 chopped zucchini

1 chopped onion (70 g)

1 sliced bell pepper

1 tsp chili powder

2 minced garlic cloves

1 tbsp. of olive oil

1 tbsp. of sesame seeds

1 tsp. of nigella seeds (optional)

10 chopped basil leaves

STEPS:

1. Add your tomatoes and onion to a large pan, cover with a lid, and cook over medium-high heat for 3–4 minutes

2. Add chickpeas and stir. Put the lid back on, and let it simmer for 5 minutes.

3. Add garlic, zucchini, and bell pepper. Stir, cover, and cook for 2 minutes.

4. Turn off the heat, add basil and olive oil, and sprinkle with sesame and nigella seeds and chili powder on top.

NUTRITIONAL INFORMATION (PER SERVING)

Calories: 446, Carbs: 66g, Protein: 20g, Fat: 14g, Fiber: 18g, Sugar: 19g

ITALIAN LENTIL SOUP

Servings: 3

Prep Time: 10 minutes

Cook Time: 25 minutes

INGREDIENTS:

2 cups (60 g) of fresh spinach / 1.5 cups of frozen spinach, thawed

2 onions (140 g)

⅓ cup (60 g) dry, coarse bulgur

½ cup (100 g) red lentils, soaked

1 potato / 2 small beets (optional)

½ red pepper

½ tsp. of turmeric

1 tbsp. of ground ginger

½ tsp. of cumin

1 tbsp. of paprika (optional)

1 garlic clove

freshly ground pepper, to taste

fresh mint leaves

2 tbsp. of olive oil

sea salt, to taste

STEPS:

1. Rinse and drain lentils and bulgur.

2. Peel and chop potato / beets if using.

3. Chop onion, mince your garlic, mince red pepper, and chop mint.

4. Add one tablespoon of olive oil, minced garlic, and chopped onion to a pot, and cook over medium-high heat for 1 minute.

5. Add spices and a few tablespoons of water.

6. Add lentils, bulgur, spinach, red pepper, mint, 2½ cups of water, and potatoes / beets. The water should be covering everything. Cover with a lid and cook for 25–30 minutes. Check on it periodically, and add more water when needed.

7. Turn off the heat, and add one tablespoon of olive oil. Serve and enjoy.

NUTRITIONAL INFORMATION (PER SERVING)

Calories: 290, Carbs: 43g, Protein: 12g, Fat: 11g, Fiber: 12g, Sugar: 9g

HOMEMADE CHICKEN SOUP

Servings: 4

Prep Time: 10 minutes

Cook Time: 40 minutes

INGREDIENTS:

1 lb. (450 g) bone-in chicken thighs

1 peeled and chopped potato

1 chopped carrot

1 chopped onion (70 g)

2 tbsp. of dried mint

1 tbsp. of turmeric

1 tbsp. of grated ginger

½ cup of chopped cauliflower

STEPS:

1. Cook chicken with 4–5 cups of water in a pot. Once the water begins boiling, add onion, potato, turmeric, and mint. Cover with a lid, and let it cook over medium-high heat for 20–30 minutes.

2. Transfer the chicken to a plate, and cool down for a few minutes.

3. Take the meat off the bone, and shred it using two forks.

4. Return the chicken to the pot. Add carrot, ginger, cauliflower, sea salt, and pepper to taste. Cook for 5–10 minutes. Serve and enjoy.

NUTRITIONAL INFORMATION (PER SERVING)

Calories: 305, Carbs: 14g, Protein: 29g, Fat: 16g, Fiber: 2g, Sugar: 2g

FISH CASSEROLE

Servings: 6

Prep Time: 10 minutes

Cook Time: 15 minutes

INGREDIENTS:

1½ lb. (675 g) white fish fillet (such as halibut or cod)

sea salt, to taste

freshly ground pepper, to taste

olive oil

1 lemon

8 oz. (230 g) halved cherry tomatoes

3 oz. (85 g) pitted and halved olives

3 tbsp. minced red onion

4–5 minced garlic cloves

1 tbsp. of fresh thyme

2 tsp. of dried oregano

STEPS:

1. Preheat your oven to 425°F (220°C). Brush a baking dish with olive oil.

2. Pat fish dry with a paper towel. Season with sea salt and pepper all over.

3. Place the fish in your baking dish, and squeeze juice from half a lemon.

4. Mix your olives, tomatoes, onions, garlic, a pinch of sea salt and pepper, 3 tablespoons of olive oil, and spices in a bowl.

5. Pour tomato mixture over the fish.

6. Bake for 15–20 minutes. At the 15-minute mark, check if the fish is done by inserting a fork and twisting. If the fish easily flakes, it is done. Remove from the oven, and serve.

NUTRITIONAL INFORMATION (PER SERVING)

Calories: 128, Carbs: 3.9g, Protein: 21g, Fat: 3g, Fiber: 1.3g

SHRIMP STEW

Servings: 6

Prep Time: 10 minutes

Cook Time: 25 minutes

INGREDIENTS:

8 oz. (230 g) scallops (optional)

1½ lb. (675 g) peeled and deveined shrimp

1 chopped green bell pepper

1 chopped red bell pepper

1 chopped yellow onion (70 g)

6 minced garlic cloves

3 tbsp. of tomato paste

1 tbsp. of dried oregano

7 cups (1.7 L) of low-sodium chicken or vegetable broth

3 diced tomatoes

1 cup (112 g) of whole-wheat orzo, cooked

6 oz. (170 g) spinach

1 cup of chopped parsley

1 cup of chopped dill

juice from 1 lemon

red pepper flakes (optional)

crusty bread (for serving, whole-wheat preferred)

sea salt, to taste

freshly ground pepper, to taste

olive oil

STEPS:

1. Pat your scallops dry and season with sea salt and pepper (if using).

2. Heat 1 tablespoon of olive oil in a cast-iron skillet over medium-high heat. Add your scallops, and sear for two minutes per side until they form a golden-brown crust. Sprinkle with a pinch of oregano, transfer them to a plate, and set them aside.

3. Add another tablespoon of olive oil, and add shrimp. Sear for 2 minutes per side (they should not be fully cooked at this point). Remove from the heat, and sprinkle with a pinch of oregano.

4. Heat one tablespoon of olive oil in a pot over medium-high heat. Add bell peppers, onions, garlic, tomato paste, the rest of your oregano, and a pinch of sea salt. Cook for 5 minutes, stirring occasionally.

5. Pour in your broth and bring it to a boil. Add diced tomatoes, and cook for 3–5 minutes.

6. Add spinach, dill, lemon juice, and parsley.

7. Add scallops and shrimp, stirring for 1–2 minutes. Remove from heat.

8. Season to taste. Add red pepper flakes, and serve with orzo pasta.

NUTRITIONAL INFORMATION (PER SERVING)

Calories: 307, Carbs: 32g, Protein: 27.4g, Fat: 10.4g, Sugar: 7g

GNOCCHI WITH ROASTED VEGGIES

Servings: 4

Prep Time: 10 minutes

Cook Time: 20 minutes

INGREDIENTS:

1 bag (1 lb. / 450 g) frozen gnocchi / cauliflower gnocchi

4 bell peppers, halved lengthwise

1 zucchini, sliced

1 ear of corn, shucked

1 cup champignons

8 cherry tomatoes

2 red onions, cut into chunks

juice from ½ lemon

2 tbsp. of avocado oil

1 tsp. of sea salt

1 tsp. of freshly ground pepper

STEPS:

1. Place an oven rack in the top position. Preheat your oven to 425°F (220°C). Line a large baking pan with foil.

2. Add all of your ingredients, minus the gnocchi, to a large bowl, and mix to combine.

3. Transfer your mixture to the baking pan.

4. Add gnocchi, spreading everything out evenly.

5. Place the baking pan in your oven and roast for 10–15 minutes. Remove it from the oven, give it a stir, and then roast for another 5–10 minutes.

6. Serve and enjoy.

NUTRITIONAL INFORMATION (PER SERVING)

Calories: 220, Carbs: 27.8g, Protein: 4g, Fat: 8.9g, Fiber: 7.4g

SANDWICHES, PIZZAS, AND WRAPS

SALMON WRAPS

Servings: 4

Prep Time: 15 minutes

Cook Time: 15 minutes

INGREDIENTS:

6 minced garlic cloves

12 oz. (340 g) salmon fillets

1½ tsp. of dried basil

½ tsp. of freshly ground pepper

sea salt, to taste

2 chopped cucumbers, plus ½ minced cucumber

⅓ cup (60 g) of olives

2 tbsp. of pickled jalapeño slices (optional)

4 tbsp. of chopped parsley

1 chopped tomato

1 cup of arugula

juice from ½ of a lemon

1 tsp. of olive oil

1 cup (240 ml) Greek yogurt

4 spinach tortillas / flatbread (for serving)

STEPS:

1. Rub the salmon with basil, 2 minced garlic cloves, and pepper. Cook in a pan for 5–6 minutes per side, or until golden brown all over. Transfer to a plate and break up the salmon into bite-sized pieces.

2. Mix yogurt, minced cucumber, a pinch of sea salt, and 3 of your minced garlic cloves in a small bowl.

3. Add chopped cucumbers, avocado, arugula, parsley, lemon juice, jalapeño (if using), olives, olive oil, a pinch of sea salt, and 1 minced garlic clove to another bowl. Mix to combine.

4. Fill a tortilla / flatbread with some tzatziki, salad, and salmon. Wrap and serve.

NUTRITIONAL INFORMATION (PER SERVING)

Calories: 567, Carbs: 55g, Protein: 31g, Fat: 25g, Fiber: 7g, Sugar: 7g

CHICKEN PITA SANDWICH

Servings: 1

Prep Time: 10 minutes

Cook Time: 10 minutes

INGREDIENTS:

1 tbsp. lemon juice

1 boneless, skinless chicken breast

sea salt, to taste

freshly ground pepper, to taste

1 whole-grain pita

arugula leaves

½ cup (60 g) grated hard cheese

1 diced tomato

1 tbsp. of chopped parsley

1 tbsp. of tahini (optional)

STEPS:

1. Squeeze lemon juice all over your chicken breast and rub in a pinch or two of sea salt and pepper.

2. Place your chicken breast on a grill or pan and cook over medium-high heat for 10–15 minutes.

3. Remove from heat, and let it cool for about 5 minutes before cutting your chicken breast into strips.

4. Cut your pita in half, making two pockets.

5. Fill each pocket with arugula, chicken, tomato, parsley, and grated cheese.

6. Drizzle with tahini (if using).

NUTRITIONAL INFORMATION (PER SERVING)

Calories: 320, Carbs: 38g, Protein: 34g, Fat: 4.5g, Fiber: 5g, Sugar: 5g

PORK WRAPS

Servings: 4

Prep Time: 15 minutes

Cook Time: 15 minutes

INGREDIENTS:

4 cups (1 Kg) cooked and shredded pork

1 cup (120 g) of crumbled feta cheese

½ cup (120 ml) of Greek yogurt

½ cup of patted dry and chopped jarred roasted red peppers

½ cup of sliced red onion

1 tsp lemon zest

2 tsp lemon juice

½ tsp. of sea salt

¼ tsp. of freshly ground pepper

4 whole-wheat tortillas

4 cups (120 g) of lettuce or spinach

STEPS:

1. Mix your pork, feta, red peppers, onion slices, yogurt, lemon juice and zest, sea salt, and pepper in a large bowl.

2. In each tortilla, arrange some lettuce and your chicken mixture. Roll tightly, slice in half, and serve.

NUTRITIONAL INFORMATION (PER SERVING)

Calories: 449, Carbs: 20g, Protein: 45g, Fat: 20g, Fiber: 2g, Sugar: 4g

SALMON CHEESE WRAPS

Servings: 3

Prep Time: 15 minutes

Cook Time: 5 minutes

7 oz. (200 g) smoked salmon slices

1 cup (240 ml) cream cheese

2 minced garlic cloves

½ tsp. of dried mint

1 tbsp. of lemon juice

1 tsp. of red pepper flakes

1 tbsp. of olive oil

½ cup (15 g) of spinach

½ cup of diced red onion

4 tortillas / pita wraps

STEPS:

1. Mix cream cheese, lemon juice, dried mint, red pepper flakes, and garlic. Add 1–2 tablespoons of water until your sauce reaches your desired level of creaminess.

2. Add some spinach, 2–3 tablespoons of sauce, and 2–3 onion slices to a tortilla to assemble the wraps. Spread 1 tablespoon of sauce over everything, and wrap the tortilla up tightly.

3. Store your ingredients separately for meal prepping.

NUTRITIONAL INFORMATION (PER SERVING)

Calories: 485, Carbs: 66g, Protein: 16g, Fat: 19g, Fiber: 11g, Sugar: 7g

LOADED VEGAN PIZZA

Servings: 8

Prep Time: 10 minutes

Cook Time: 30 minutes

INGREDIENTS:

1 batch of pizza dough

1 tbsp. of olive oil

2 tsp. of minced garlic

1½ cups (170 g) of shredded mozzarella

2 cups (60 g) of spinach

6–8 sliced grape tomatoes

¼ cup (45 g) of sliced black olives

1 cup of quartered artichokes

½ red onion, sliced

½ cup (60 g) of crumbled feta cheese

chopped parsley

STEPS:

1. Preheat your oven to 400°F (205°C).

2. Bake pizza dough for 8 minutes. Remove from the oven and drizzle with olive oil.

3. Add garlic, mozzarella, spinach, tomatoes, olives, artichokes, red onion, and feta. Sprinkle with parsley.

4. Bake for 15–20 minutes.

5. Let it cool for 5–10 minutes before slicing and serving.

NUTRITIONAL INFORMATION (PER SERVING)

Calories: 296, Carbs: 30g, Protein: 11g, Fat: 15g, Fiber: 4g, Sugar: 3g

MARGHERITA PIZZA

Servings: 8

Prep Time: 10 minutes

Cook Time: 18 minutes

INGREDIENTS:

whole-wheat pizza crust

2 tbsp. of olive oil

½ cup of canned crushed / diced tomatoes, with most of the liquid drained

½ cup (60 g) of grated mozzarella cheese

12 basil leaves

3—4 sliced Roma tomatoes

STEPS:

1. Preheat your oven to 425°F (220°C). Place a pizza stone in the middle of your oven rack.

2. Place a large sheet of parchment paper on a counter. Roll out your pizza crust to the desired thickness.

3. Spread about 1 tablespoon of olive oil over the crust.

4. Spread canned tomatoes on the crust so they reach ½ inch (1.3 cm) away from the crust's edge.

5. Sprinkle cheese all over.

6. Top your pizza off with the rest of the ingredients.

7. Use parchment paper to transfer the pizza onto the pizza stone in the oven.

8. Bake for 15–18 minutes, or until the crust begins to brown and everything appears done. Remove from the oven, slice into 8 slices, and serve.

NUTRITIONAL INFORMATION (PER SERVING)

Calories: 250, Carbs: 30g, Fat: 12.8g, Fiber: 3g

PANINI WITH FETA CHEESE

Servings: 1

Prep Time: 5 minutes

Cook Time: 5 minutes

INGREDIENTS:

2 slices of whole-wheat Italian bread

1 tsp unsalted butter

2 slices of feta cheese

¼ cup of kale

3 red onion slices

1 slice of tomato

2 tbsp. of black olives

1 tbsp. ground beef, cooked

STEPS:

1. Heat a skillet. Butter one side of both slices of bread and place them butter-side down on the skillet.

2. Add your kale, beef, cheese, onions, tomato, and olives to one slice of bread, and place the other slice of bread on top of everything.

3. Grill on both sides until the cheese has melted.

NUTRITIONAL INFORMATION (PER SERVING)

Calories: 438, Carbs: 31.6g, Protein: 20g, Fat: 26.2g, Fiber: 7g, Sugar: 7g

DESSERTS

PEAR CRUMBLE

Servings: 2

Prep Time: 5 minutes

Cook Time: 10 minutes

INGREDIENTS:

2 tsp. of cinnamon

sea salt, to taste

2½ tbsp. of coconut oil

1 tbsp. liquid honey, plus more for serving

1½ tbsp. of shredded coconut

2 pears

½ cup (40 g) of oats

¼ cup of nuts

STEPS:

1. Place oats, nuts, shredded coconut, honey, 1½ tablespoon of coconut oil, 1 tablespoon of water, 1 tablespoon of cinnamon, and a pinch or two of sea salt in a food processor. Process until it reaches the consistency of a crumble.

2. Heat ½ tablespoon coconut oil in a pan, and add your crumble. Cook for 5 minutes, stirring occasionally. Remove from heat.

3. Chop your pears into cubes.

4. Place the rest of your coconut oil, cinnamon, and pears in another pan and sauté for 3–4 minutes over medium heat.

5. Place your pear mixture and crumble mixture in a bowl and drizzle with more honey.

NUTRITIONAL INFORMATION (PER SERVING)

Calories: 488, Carbs: 57g, Protein: 7g, Fat: 29g, Fiber: 11g, Sugar: 28g

LEMON CAKE

Servings: 10

Prep Time: 1 hour, 10 minutes

Cook Time: 42 minutes

INGREDIENTS:

2 cups (225 g) of almond flour

¾ cup (90 g) of polenta

1½ tsp. of baking powder

¼ tsp. of sea salt

7 oz. (200 g) unsalted butter, plus more

1 cup of granulated white sugar

3 whole eggs

zest from 2 lemons

½ tsp. of vanilla extract

½ cup of powdered sugar

3 tbsp. of lemon juice

whipped cream (optional for serving)

STEPS:

1. Preheat your oven to 350°F (176°C). Line a 9-inch (23 cm) round cake pan with parchment paper and coat with some butter.

2. Combine almond flour, polenta, sea salt, and baking powder in a bowl.

3. Whisk together sugar and butter in a large bowl using an electric mixer. Beat for about 3 minutes on medium speed, so the mixture lightens in color.

4. Add ⅓ of your flour mixture to the butter mixture and continue beating on medium speed until everything is mixed well. Add an egg and continue to beat. Continue adding the flour mixture in thirds, alternating with your eggs.

5. Add lemon zest and vanilla extract and beat to combine.

6. Transfer your batter to the cake pan, spreading it out evenly.

7. Bake for 40 minutes, or until the cake's edges start to separate from the sides of the pan.

8. Remove the cake from the oven and place it on a wire rack to cool.

9. Add powdered sugar and lemon juice to a saucepan over low heat. Cook, occasionally stirring, until the sugar is dissolved. Remove from heat.

10. Use a toothpick to poke the cake about 1 inch (2.5 cm) apart. Drizzle syrup mixture all over the cake.

11. Finish letting the cake cool completely (this should take about 1½ hours).

12. Cut your cake and serve with whipped cream (if using).

NUTRITIONAL INFORMATION (PER SERVING)

Calories: 444, Carbs: 41.3g, Protein: 8g, Fat: 29g, Fiber: 3.1g, Sugar: 27.3g

HONEY CAKE

Servings: 12

Prep Time: 20 minutes

Cook Time: 40 minutes

INGREDIENTS:

1 cup (240 ml) of Greek yogurt

⅔ cup (160 ml) olive oil, plus more

⅔ cup (160 ml) liquid honey

1 tbsp. of chopped thyme

1 tsp. of lemon zest

3 whole eggs

1½ cups (200 g) of all-purpose flour

½ tsp. of baking powder

½ tsp. of baking soda

¼ tsp. of sea salt

Strawberry slices (optional for serving)

STEPS:

1. Heat your oven to 325°F (163°C). Line a 9-inch (23 cm) round cake pan with parchment paper and coat with olive oil.

2. Whisk together yogurt, olive oil, honey, thyme, and lemon zest in a large bowl. Beat your eggs in one at a time. Add flour, baking powder, baking soda, and sea salt. Mix until the batter is almost smooth.

3. Spread your batter into the cake pan evenly.

4. Bake for 40–45 minutes, until the top of the cake is lightly browned. Use a toothpick to check if the cake is done by sticking it in the center. If it comes out clean, the cake is done. If it does not, let it bake for a few more minutes.

5. Transfer the cake to a cooling rack for 10 minutes before taking it out of the pan. Serve warm or at room temperature and top with strawberries (if using).

NUTRITIONAL INFORMATION (PER SERVING)

Calories: 260, Carbs: 28.5g, Protein: 5g, Fat: 14.6g, Fiber: 0.6g, Sugar: 16.4g

CREAMY CHOCOLATE MOUSSE

Servings: 4

Prep Time: 5 minutes

Cook Time: 10 minutes

INGREDIENTS:

1¼ cups (300 ml) almond milk / coconut milk

1 lb. (450 g) of chopped dark chocolate

4 chopped avocados

¼ cup (60 ml) of agave

1 tbsp. of orange zest

2 tbsp. of puffed quinoa

½ tsp. of sea salt

2 tsp. of blueberries

STEPS:

1. Heat your milk over medium-high heat in a saucepan until it reaches 175°F (80°C) on an instant-read thermometer. Remove from heat and stir in the chopped chocolate until it has melted. Set aside to cool.

2. Place avocados, agave, orange zest, and cooled chocolate mixture in a blender. Blend on high until everything is smooth.

3. Sprinkle with puffed quinoa and serve with berries.

NUTRITIONAL INFORMATION (PER SERVING)

Calories: 596, Carbs: 92g, Protein: 26g, Fat: 42g, Sugar: 12g

SWEET PEANUT BUTTER COOKIES

Servings: 14

Prep Time: 20 minutes

Cook Time: 10 minutes

INGREDIENTS:

½ cup of roasted and sea salted peanuts

2 tbsp. of light brown sugar

1 cup (240 g) of peanut butter

⅔ cup (160 g) of coconut sugar

1 medium banana, mashed

2 tbsp. of maple syrup

2 tsp. of vanilla extract

½ tsp. of baking soda

½ tsp. of sea salt

STEPS:

1. Preheat your oven to 375°F (190°C). Line two baking sheets with parchment paper.

2. Chop your peanuts. Set aside half of them, and keep chopping the rest until they are finely chopped. Place the finely chopped peanuts in a small bowl and add sugar. Set aside.

3. Mix reserved coarsely chopped peanuts, peanut butter, sea salt, baking soda, vanilla, syrup, banana, and coconut sugar in a bowl until your mixture is sticky and thick. Let it sit for 15 minutes.

4. Place one large scoop of dough into the bowl with the finely chopped peanuts and roll around to coat. Form the dough into a ball and place it on the baking sheet, flattening it into a thick cookie shape. Repeat for the rest of the dough.

5. Bake for 8–10 minutes. Let them cool for 10 minutes before serving.

NUTRITIONAL INFORMATION (PER SERVING)

Calories: 185, Carbs: 18g, Protein: 5g, Fat: 11g, Sugar: 15g

NO-BAKE SNACK BARS

Servings: 8

Prep Time: 2 hours, 15 minutes

Total Time: 2 hours, 15 minutes

INGREDIENTS:

2⅓ cups of pitted dates

1⅓ cups of almonds

⅓ cup plus ¼ cup of cocoa powder

2 tsp. of vanilla extract

¼ tsp. of sea salt

1 cup of blueberries

1 cup of roughly chopped macadamia nuts

¼ cup (60 ml) of maple syrup

2 tbsp. of melted coconut oil

STEPS:

1. Grease an 8-inch (20 cm) square baking pan and line it with parchment paper.

2. Add dates, almonds, ⅓cup of cocoa powder, 1 tablespoon of water, vanilla extract, and sea salt to a food processor and process until everything is smooth. Spread out your mixture evenly into the pan.

3. Sprinkle blueberries and macadamia nuts over everything and lightly press them into the batter.

4. Mix coconut oil, syrup, and ¼ cup of cocoa powder in a bowl. Pour your mixture over the batter, spreading it out evenly.

5. Place the pan in the fridge. Let it chill for at least 2 hours before serving.

NUTRITIONAL INFORMATION (PER SERVING)

Calories: 592, Carbs: 83g, Protein: 10g, Fat: 31g, Sugar: 65g

SAUCES & DRESSINGS

GREEK SALAD DRESSING

Servings: 12

Prep Time: 5 minutes

Total Time: 5 minutes

INGREDIENTS:

¾ cup (180 ml) of olive oil

zest from 1 lemon

juice from 1 lemon (about ¼ cup)

¼ cup (60 ml) of red wine vinegar

1 tsp. of Dijon mustard

1 tsp. of dried oregano

1 minced garlic clove

¼ cup (30 g) of crumbled feta (optional)

sea salt, to taste

freshly ground pepper, to taste

STEPS:

1. Place olive oil, lemon zest and juice, vinegar, mustard, oregano, and garlic in a jar.

2. Seal the jar and shake vigorously. Add your feta (if using), and shake again.

3. Season with sea salt and pepper to taste.

NUTRITIONAL INFORMATION (PER SERVING)

Calories: 132, Carbs: 1g, Protein: 1g, Fat: 14g, Fiber: 1g, Sugar: 1g

TAHINI LEMON GARLIC SAUCE

Servings: 8

Prep Time: 10 minutes

Total Time: 10 minutes

INGREDIENTS:

3 garlic cloves

½ cup (120 g) of tahini

¼ cup (60 ml) of lemon juice

1 tbsp. of olive oil

sea salt, to taste

freshly ground pepper, to taste

STEPS:

1. Mince your garlic in a food processor.

2. Add your tahini, olive oil, and lemon juice to the food processor, and mince for 10 seconds.

3. Add 4 tablespoons of water to the food processor, processing 1 tablespoon at a time until the mixture reaches your desired consistency.

4. Season with sea salt and pepper to taste.

NUTRITIONAL INFORMATION (PER SERVING)

Calories: 108, Carbs: 4g, Protein: 3g, Fat: 10g, Fiber: 1g, Sugar: 1g

SMOOTH YOGURT SAUCE

Servings: 12

Prep Time: 5 minutes

Total Time: 5 minutes

INGREDIENTS:

1 cup (240 ml) of Greek yogurt

2 tbsp. of Sriracha

1 tsp. of paprika

2 peeled garlic cloves

¼ tsp. of sea salt

¼ tsp. of freshly ground pepper

STEPS:

1. Place your garlic in a food processor to dice, and blitz it for 2–3 seconds.
2. Add yogurt, paprika, Sriracha, sea salt, and pepper. Blitz for 2–3 more seconds.
3. Scrape your mixture off the sides of the food processor and blitz for 2 seconds.
4. Transfer to a bowl and serve.

NUTRITIONAL INFORMATION (PER SERVING)

Calories: 11, Carbs: 1g, Protein: 2g, Fat: 1g, Fiber: 1g, Sugar: 1g

EGGPLANT BABA GANOUSH

Servings: 8

Prep Time: 20 minutes

Cook Time: 40 minutes

INGREDIENTS:

1 large eggplant, cut into 1-inch (2.5 cm) cubes

3 tbsp. of olive oil

½ tsp. of sea salt

½ cup (120 ml) of Greek yogurt

2 tbsp. of tahini

2 tsp. of lemon juice

¼ tsp. of cumin

¼ tsp. of freshly ground pepper

1 thinly sliced garlic clove

STEPS:

1. Preheat your oven to 400°F (205°C). Line a baking sheet with foil.

2. Mix cubed eggplant, 2 tablespoons of olive oil, and ¼ teaspoon of sea salt together in a large bowl. Arrange your mixture on your baking sheet.

3. Roast for 20 minutes, mix everything up, and roast for 20 more minutes.

4. Remove from the oven and let it sit for 10 minutes.

5. Transfer your eggplant to a food processor and pulse 8–10 times so the eggplant is finely chopped.

6. Transfer eggplant to a bowl and add yogurt, tahini, lemon juice, cumin, pepper, and the rest of the sea salt. Mix well to combine.

7. Heat 1 tablespoon of oil in a skillet over medium-low heat. Add your garlic and cook for about 4 minutes, so it is golden and just starting to get crispy.

8. Transfer garlic with the oil to a small bowl, and let it sit for 2 minutes to cool off before transferring it to the eggplant dip.

NUTRITIONAL INFORMATION (PER SERVING)

Calories: 103, Carbs: 5.7g, Protein: 2.8g, Fat: 8.2g, Fiber: 2.1g, Sugar: 2.8g

LEMON PISTACHIO LABNEH DIP

Servings: 8

Prep Time: 15 minutes

Total Time: 12 hours

INGREDIENTS:

4 cups (1 L) of low-fat Greek yogurt

¼ tsp. of sea salt

¼ cup of shelled pistachios

1 tbsp. of olive oil

1 tbsp. of chopped parsley

1 tsp. of lemon zest

¼ tsp. of ground sumac

STEPS:

1. Line a large mesh sieve with four layers of cheesecloth. Place it over a deep bowl so that you have 3 inches of space between the sieve and the bottom of the bowl.

2. Whisk your yogurt and sea salt in a bowl. Transfer the mixture to the cheesecloth.

3. Refrigerate for 12–24 hours.

4. Discard the liquid that has drained into the bowl.

5. Sprinkle pistachios, olive oil, parsley, lemon zest, and sumac over your dip and serve.

NUTRITIONAL INFORMATION (PER SERVING)

Calories: 108, Carbs: 8.3g, Protein: 7g, Fat: 5.3g, Fiber: 0.4g

BREAD

BREAD WITH BLACK OLIVES

Prep Time: 30 minutes

Rising Time: 1 hour 40 minutes

Cooking Time: 45 minutes

Servings: 6

INGREDIENTS:

3 cups (390 g) of all-purpose flour

2 tsp. active dry yeast

2 tbsp. white sugar

1 tsp. sea salt

½ cup (90 g) black olives, chopped

3 tbsp. olive oil

1¼ cups (300 ml) of warm water (about 110°F / 43°C)

1 tbsp. cornmeal

STEPS:

1. In a large bowl, combine flour, sugar, yeast, sea salt, black olives, water, and olive oil.

2. Mix well to prepare the dough.

3. Turn the dough onto a floured surface and knead well for 5-10 minutes until elastic.

4. Set dough aside and allow it to rise for about 45 minutes until it has doubled in size.

5. Punch the dough down and knead again for 10 minutes.

6. Allow it to rise for 30 minutes more.

7. Round the dough on a kneading board, place it upside down in a bowl, and line it with a lint-free, well-floured towel.

8. Allow it to rise until it has doubled in size again.

9. While the bread rises for the third and final time, take a pan, fill it with water, and place it at the bottom of your oven.

10. Preheat the oven to a temperature of 500°F (260°C).

11. Turn the loaf onto a sheet pan, lightly oil it, and dust it with cornmeal.

12. Bake for about 15 minutes.

13. Reduce heat to 375°F (190°C) and bake for another 30 minutes.

NUTRITIONAL INFORMATION (PER SERVING)

Calories: 324, Total Fat: 8.9 g, Saturated Fat: 1.3 g, Cholesterol: 0 mg, Sodium: 488 mg, Total Carbohydrate: 53.9 g, Dietary Fiber: 2.4 g, Total Sugars: 4.2 g, Protein: 7.2 g, Vitamin D: 0 mcg, Calcium: 20 mg, Iron: 4 mg, Potassium: 98 mg

CHEESY BREAD

Prep Time: 5 minutes

Cooking Time: 15 minutes

Servings: 12

3 cups (340 g) shredded cheddar cheese

1 cup (240 ml) mayonnaise

1 1-oz. (28 g) pack dry ranch dressing mix

1 2-oz. can (60 g) chopped black olives, drained

4 green onions, sliced

2 French baguettes, cut into ½-inch (1.3 cm) slices

STEPS:

1. Preheat the oven to 350°F (177°C).
2. In a medium-sized bowl, combine cheese, ranch dressing mix, mayonnaise, onions, and olives.
3. Increase mayo if you want a juicier mixture.
4. Spread cheese mixture on top of your French baguette slices.
5. Arrange the slices in a single layer on a large baking sheet.
6. Bake for about 15 minutes until the cheese is bubbly and browning.
7. Serve warm!

NUTRITIONAL INFORMATION (PER SERVING)

Calories: 290, Total Fat: 17 g, Saturated Fat: 7.2 g, Cholesterol: 35 mg, Sodium: 578 mg, Total Carbohydrate: 23.9 g, Dietary Fiber: 1.1 g, Total Sugars: 2.4 g, Protein: 11.1 g, Vitamin D: 3 mcg, Calcium: 229 mg, Iron: 2 mg, Potassium: 85 mg

CHEESY OLIVE BREAD

Prep Time: 10 minutes

Cooking Time: 15 minutes

Servings: 8

INGREDIENTS:

½ cup (120 g) softened butter

¼ cup (60 ml) mayo

1 tsp. garlic powder

1 tsp. onion powder

2 cups (230 g) shredded mozzarella cheese

½ cup (90 g) chopped black olives

1 loaf of French Bread, halved longways

STEPS:

1. Preheat the oven to a temperature of 350°F (177°C).

2. Stir butter and mayo together in a bowl until it is smooth and creamy.

3. Add onion powder, garlic powder, olives, and cheese and stir.

4. Spread the mixture over French bread.

5. Place bread on a baking sheet and bake for 10-12 minutes.

6. Increase the heat to broil and cook until the cheese has melted and the bread is golden brown.

7. Pre-heat before eating.

NUTRITIONAL INFORMATION (PER SERVING)

Calories: 307, Total Fat: 17.7 g, Saturated Fat: 9.2 g, Cholesterol: 38 mg, Sodium: 482 mg, Total Carbohydrate: 30.1 g, Dietary Fiber: 1.5 g, Total Sugars: 1.9 g, Protein: 8 g, Vitamin D: 0 mcg, Calcium: 40 mg, Iron: 2 mg, Potassium: 73 mg

ITALIAN HERB BREAD

Prep Time: 20 minutes

Rising Time: 2 hours

Cooking Time: 40 minutes

Servings: 25

INGREDIENTS:

1 2/3 tsp. active dry yeast

3½ cups (455 g) of all-purpose flour

2 1/4 cups (300 g) rye flour

1 tbsp. sea salt

2 tbsp. olive oil

1 tbsp. flat-leaf parsley, finely chopped

10 sprigs fresh thyme leaves, stems removed

1 garlic clove, peeled and finely chopped

¼ cup (45 g) black olives, pitted and chopped

3 green chilies, deseeded and chopped

¾ cup (100 g) sun-dried tomatoes, drained and chopped

STEPS:

1. Take a bowl of lukewarm water (100°F / 38°C) and dissolve the yeast.

2. Add flour, yeast water, and sea salt to another bowl.

3. Mix well to prepare the dough using a mixer or your hands.

4. Put the dough in a large, clean bowl and allow it to rest covered for 2 hours.

5. Transfer dough to a lightly floured surface and knead, adding parsley, garlic, olives, thyme, tomatoes, and chilies.

6. Place the kneaded dough in an 8½-inch (22 cm) bread basket.

7. Cover and allow to rest for about 60 minutes.

8. Preheat the oven to 400°F (205°C).

9. Bake for about 30-40 minutes.

NUTRITIONAL INFORMATION (PER SERVING)

Calories: 338, Total Fat: 2.5 g, Saturated Fat: 0.4 g, Cholesterol: 0 mg, Sodium: 294 mg, Total Carbohydrate: 68.6 g, Dietary Fiber: 5.5 g, Total Sugars: 0.5 g, Protein: 10 g, Vitamin D: 0 mcg, Calcium: 53 mg, Iron: 7 mg, Potassium: 202 mg

MEDITERRANEAN FOCACCIA

Prep Time: 30 minutes

Rising Time: 1½ hours

Cooking Time: 30 minutes

Servings: 4

INGREDIENTS:

3 3/5 cups (470 g) all-purpose flour

1 1/7 cups (280 ml) lukewarm water

2 tbsp. olive oil

2 tsp. active dry yeast

1½ tsp. sea sea salt

1 cup (180 g) green olives, pitted and coarsely chopped

coarse sea salt, for sprinkling

olive oil

STEPS:

1. Place flour and yeast in a large bowl.

2. Make a well and pour in water, sea salt, and oil.

3. Gradually keep mixing until everything is incorporated well.

4. Knead for about 20 minutes.

5. Add black olives and mix well.

6. Form a ball and allow it to rise for about 45 minutes (in a bowl covered with a towel).

7. Once the dough is ready, push air out of it by crushing it using your palm.

8. Roll out the dough onto a floured surface to a thickness of about ½ an inch.

9. Place it on a baking sheet covered with parchment paper, and allow the dough to rise for another 45 minutes.

10. Preheat the oven to 425°F (218°C).

11. Press fingers into the dough at regular intervals to pierce the dough.

12. When ready to bake, pour some olive oil into the holes and sprinkle with sea salt.

13. Bake for 20-30 minutes.

NUTRITIONAL INFORMATION (PER SERVING)

Calories: 523, Total Fat: 11.7 g, Saturated Fat: 1.7 g, Cholesterol: 0 mg, Sodium: 3495 mg, Total Carbohydrate: 89.4 g, Dietary Fiber: 4.6 g, Total Sugars: 0.3 g, Protein: 13.8 g, Vitamin D: 0 mcg, Calcium: 50 mg, Iron: 7 mg, Potassium: 124 mg

OLIVE FOUGASSE

Prep Time: 10 minutes

Resting Time: 1½ hours

Cooking Time: 20 minutes

Servings: 4

INGREDIENTS:

3 2/3 cups (470 g) bread flour

3 1/2 tbsp. olive oil

1 2/3 tbsp. bread yeast

1 1/4 cups (225 g) black olives, chopped (optional)

1 tsp. oregano

1 tsp. sea salt

1 cup (240 ml) water

STEPS:

1. Add flour to a bowl.

2. Make a well in the center and add the water and remaining ingredients.

3. Knead the dough until it becomes slightly elastic.

4. Mold it into a ball and let it stand for about 1 hour.

5. Divide the dough into four pieces of equal portions.

6. Flatten the balls using a rolling pin and place them on a floured baking tray.

7. Make incisions on the bread.

8. Allow them to rest for about 30 minutes

9. Preheat the oven to 425°F (218°C).

10. Brush the Fougasse with olive oil and allow it to bake for 20 minutes.

11. Turn the oven off and allow it to rest for 5 minutes.

12. Remove and allow to cool.

NUTRITIONAL INFORMATION (PER SERVING)

Calories: 586, Total Fat: 18.1 g, Saturated Fat: 2.6 g, Cholesterol: 0 mg, Sodium: 371 mg, Total Carbohydrate: 92.2 g, Dietary Fiber: 5.6 g, Total Sugars: 0.3 g, Protein: 14.2 g, Vitamin D: 0 mcg, Calcium: 63 mg, Iron: 8 mg, Potassium: 232 mg

FROM THE AUTHOR

I've been a **professional chef for over 15 years** and a passionate advocate for healthy food. My areas of expertise include **recipe development, healthy meal plans, and professional cooking.** I help people to be healthier and enjoy delicious food.

I have loved cooking since my childhood. I always collect new recipes and develop my own. First, I learned how to prepare classic dishes and then plunged into traditional European recipes. I studied the art of cooking with the best American and European chefs.

And I generously share my recipes and the secrets of mastery with my readers. Let your house be filled with the cozy smell of freshly cooked food!

Thank you, dear readers!

I am so grateful for those of you who make up the community of readers I love writing recipe books for! Thank you for your shares, encouraging emails, feedback, and reviews. I appreciate each one more than you, guys, know!

If you enjoy the book or find it useful, I kindly ask that you leave a review. Your reviews help me out SO MUCH! They inspire me to create more books for you and your family to enjoy and also help spread the word to other readers about these recipes. I greatly appreciate it. Have an amazing day!

If you have any questions, feel free to contact me

Facebook

Goodreads

OUR RECOMMENDATIONS

Vegan Meal Prep Cookbook: Beginner's Plant-Based Meal Prep to Save Your Time and Money. 7-Day Meal Plan

Bread Machine Cookbook: Delicious Recipes for Homemade Bread

Copyright

ALL ©COPYRIGHTS RESERVED 2019 by Jennifer Tate

All Rights Reserved. No part of this publication or the Information in it may be quoted from or reproduced in any form by means such as printing, scanning, photocopying, or otherwise without prior written permission of the copyright holder.

Disclaimer and Terms of Use: Effort has been made to ensure that the information in this book is accurate and complete; however, the author and the publisher do not warrant the accuracy of the information, text, or graphics contained within the book due to the rapidly changing nature of science, research, known and unknown facts, and the internet. The author and the publisher are not responsible for errors, omissions, or contrary interpretations of the subject matter herein. This book is presented solely for motivational and informational purposes only.

Made in the USA
Middletown, DE
20 October 2022

13182275R00073